ARSENAL

A RANDOM HISTORY

An exclusive edition for

for all your gift books and gift stationery

This edition first published in Great Britain in 2023 by Allsorted Ltd, Watford, Herts, UK WD19 4BG

The facts and statistics in this book are correct up to the end of the 2022/23 season. The data comes from publicly available sources and is presented as correct as far as our knowledge allows. The opinions in this book are personal and individual and are not affiliated to the football club in any way. Any views or opinions represented in this book are personal and belong solely to the book author and do not represent those of people, institutions or organisations that the football club or publisher may or may not be associated with in professional or personal capacity, unless explicitly stated. Any views or opinions are not intended to malign any religious, ethnic group, club, organisation, company or individual.

© Susanna Geoghegan Gift Publishing
Author: Magnus Allan
Cover design: Milestone Creative
Contents design: Bag of Badgers Ltd
Illustrations: Ludovic Sallé

ISBN: 978-1-915902-10-8

Printed in China

★ CONTENTS ★

"WE DON'T SIGN
SUPERSTARS, WE
MAKE THEM."

Arsène Wenger justifies Arsenal's
limited transfer window activity.

★ INTRODUCTION: ★

VICTORY THROUGH HARMONY

Arsenal are one of the most celebrated and most decorated football teams in the world. Rising from humble south London beginnings before taking the plunge, packing up their things and moving north in the early 20th century, the team has delivered an astonishing story of success.

To date, they have won 13 Premier League or First Division titles, 14 FA Cups, 16 Charity Shields, two Football League or English Football League Cups, a European Cup Winners' Cup and an Inter-Cities Fairs Cup. Admittedly, that last one is a little obscure, but they all count, and the Noel Beard Trophy is a stunning piece of silverware that would grace any mantlepiece.

But it's not just a question of what the team has won. They have proudly stood as one of the world's elite teams for an unprecedented length of time. Even in the more challenging recent years that the team has endured, they have been more likely than not to feature in the

Champions League, arguably the world's most important club football competition.

The question that most other clubs have asked is: How has Arsenal managed to stay there or thereabouts for so long? It's a complex formula, but let's try to define a few elements of the answer.

Arsenal have tended to achieve things while maintaining a relatively sensible financial approach. In a world where the global records for new signings tumble away seemingly every transfer window, this has meant that there have been seasons where the team has lacked a cutting edge, but Arsenal haven't really faced the financial cliff edge that many other clubs have stared over since before World War I (see page 38).

The team have also tended to stay more loyal to their managers than most (see page 64), giving them the time (mostly) to develop and implement their footballing philosophies rather than lurching from hire to hire in an endless quest for an identity.

This hasn't stopped Arsenal from innovating and making changes when they are necessary, most famously with the move from Woolwich to Islington more than a century ago.

We've had the leadership in place that is willing to look at a situation, spot when issues could become problems and make changes even when the medicine has hurt. Nobody really wanted to leave Highbury, but it was undoubtedly the right move to make (see page 88).

Arsenal have been one of the leading teams in the First Division and the Premier League more times than any other, and even when they are not leading, they tend to be the team that nobody else wants to face. That's a reputation and a legacy to be proud of.

RESPECT THE BADGE, ★FEAR THE CANNON★

With many clubs, there's a long story about the badge that they wear on their chest – a whole routine about how it came about, who came up with the idea and who designed it, and how it has changed down the ages.

Not with Arsenal. The clue is in the name. The team was formed by a group of Victorian lads with smart moustaches that worked in a munitions factory in south London that made cannons. And so their early crests showed three cannons, viewed from above, similar to the coat of arms of the Borough of Woolwich.

In the 1920s, the club wanted to update its identity to reflect the fact that it had moved north of the river Thames with something that looked to the future, paid respect to its past, but moved away from direct associations with Woolwich. Someone suggested that a single cannon from another angle would look good.

And it did.

The badge has evolved through the years since to reflect the fashion (and the alleged fact that no one had thought to copyright the 1920s cannon), but it's remained one of the most simple and iconic badges in the history of football. Arsenal. The Gunners. With a cannon.

ARSENAL WERE THE FIRST ENGLISH TEAM TO BEAT REAL MADRID AT SANTIAGO BERNABÉU, BAYERN MUNICH AT ALLIANZ ARENA AND AC MILAN AT SAN SIRO.

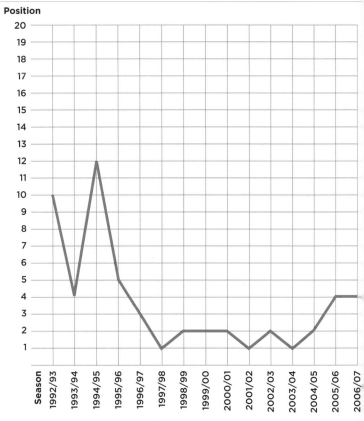

PREMIER LEAGUE
★ FINAL POSITIONS ★

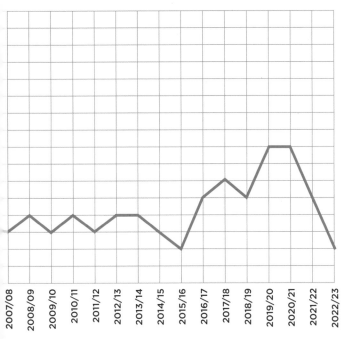

2007/08 2008/09 2009/10 2010/11 2011/12 2012/13 2013/14 2014/15 2015/16 2016/17 2017/18 2018/19 2019/20 2020/21 2021/22 2022/23

★ DAVID DANSKIN ★

Fife-born David Danskin was one of the founder members of the Dial Square Football Club. As a left-back who captained Kirkcaldy Wanderers, he'd moved down from Scotland to work in the Royal Arsenal in Woolwich, alongside two other Kirkcaldy players. Once established in the south, the Scots met a couple of former Nottingham Forest players (who still had their club jerseys), sat down with them in a pub and had the fine idea to form a football team.

Danskin was a driving force in the team's development over the first couple of years, collecting players' subs and purchasing the team's first football. He was the club's first captain, helping guide them to the semi-final of the London Association Senior Challenge Cup in 1889, although injuries regularly kept him off the pitch.

As time went on and his playing days passed, he retained a presence at the club, which presumably enabled his son to get a job selling programmes at the Manor Ground.

In later life, he moved to Warwickshire, but he was always interested in the progress of the club that he helped set up, and was said have listened to Arsenal win the FA Cup on the radio while in hospital in 1936.

★ THE PLUMSTEAD DAYS

Most of the great football teams of today did not suddenly spring up out of nowhere. Arsenal are descended from a string of amateur clubs that were set up in the 1880s, shortly after the rules of football were formalised (see page 110).

The first place that proto-Arsenal, or 'Dial Square' as the team was initially called, played at is described in the historical records as a field on the Isle of Dogs. Unbelievably, it gets less glamorous from there.

The team moved over to a field in Plumstead Marshes, which was renamed the 'Sportsman Ground' after a nearby pub that was presumably very convenient for a non-professional team. Unfortunately, and perhaps unsurprisingly, the marshes were prone to flooding, and they had to move to the nearby Manor Field.

Renaming it the 'Manor Ground', and borrowing what they could from a nearby army base so that spectators had somewhere to sit, the newly named 'Royal Arsenal' found that their new home was also prone to flooding. The issue here was that their new pitch was close to the Southern Outfall Sewer that linked to the Crossness Pumping Station, so when it flooded it sounds like things got a little grim. Let's put it like this, not even Jürgen Klinsmann would have risked a dive on the Manor Ground.

Still, after two years and potentially too many floaters in the box, the team moved to the Invicta Ground, an actual stadium in Plumstead that boasted unheard-of luxuries, such as fan terraces and player changing rooms.

Unfortunately, after two or three years, the landlords put the rent up, so the team, now called 'Woolwich Arsenal', moved back to the Manor Ground, issuing shares to fans so that they could buy the land and make it fit for purpose.

This was achieved by the 1893/94 season, and so Woolwich Arsenal made their debut in the Football League with a brand spanking new stadium that had the initial capacity to hold 6,000 people. They stayed there for the next two decades, moving from the Second Division to consolidating a place in the First Division and reaching the last four in the FA Cup twice in consecutive years.

"IT'S NOT IMPOSSIBLE TO GO THROUGH A SEASON UNBEATEN AND I CAN'T SEE WHY IT'S SHOCKING TO SAY THAT,"

suggests Arsène Wenger, attracting widespread ridicule. And then he built a team that did it. It's only hubris if you don't deliver.

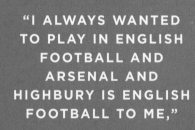

"I ALWAYS WANTED TO PLAY IN ENGLISH FOOTBALL AND ARSENAL AND HIGHBURY IS ENGLISH FOOTBALL TO ME,"

says Dennis Bergkamp, whose statue now graces the entrance to the Clock End of the Emirates Stadium.

★ EDDIE HAPGOOD ★

Eddie Hapgood was central to Arsenal's exceptional team of the 1930s. He captained the side that took the First Division title five times and lifted the FA Cup twice over the course of a decade. He's also got a decent shout at being known as the first modern footballer, supplementing his football wages with modelling and advertising campaigns for chocolate, as well as writing *Football Ambassador*, one of the first footballing autobiographies.

His early relationship with the beautiful game didn't necessarily bode well, with Hapgood finding himself up in court for smashing a window while playing in the street as a youngster, but he also played for a local Bristol team, where he caught the eye of Bristol Rovers and was offered a trial.

Rovers offered him his first contract, £8 per week as well as a job driving a coal wagon during the summer, but he turned the opportunity down and signed for non-league Kettering Town instead. Kettering only offered half the amount but would allow Hapgood to keep his job as a milkman. Milk was more glamorous that coal, it seems.

Hapgood signed for Arsenal in 1927 after 12 games with

the Poppies, and spent his first couple of years as an understudy for left-back Horace Cope. He used his time wisely, accessing the state-of-the-art facilities at Highbury and the support of the backroom staff to bulk himself up and become physically stronger. When the opportunity came to take his place in the First 11 in 1929, he stepped up and became a mainstay of the Arsenal team for the next decade. He became club captain at the start of the 1937/38 season.

He also represented England 30 times, which does not put him very high on the list of players that have represented the Three Lions, but this was during the era that England had walked away from FIFA, weren't taking part in the newly developed World Cup and there was no such thing as the Euros, so the national team was not a regular part of the footballing schedules. He was England captain 21 times, the first of which was during the infamous 'Battle of Highbury' against Italy in 1934 (see page 142), where he suffered a broken nose (one of the more minor injuries).

Hapgood's time at Arsenal ended on a sour note, unfortunately, with a disagreement around whether he was eligible for a long service bonus, despite the fact that professional football had been suspended during World War II. This isn't really the place for a debate about the rights and wrongs of this, but the relationship between team and captain never recovered.

After the war, he tried his hand at football management but didn't enjoy a great deal of success; eventually, he moved on from football entirely.

WOOLWICH ARSENAL WERE RELEGATED IN 1913 HAVING ONLY WON ONE HOME MATCH ALL SEASON.

SNAFFLING SPARE NOTTINGHAM FOREST ★ KITS ★

Once upon a time, when the world was much younger than it is today, the team that eventually became Arsenal were called 'Dial Square'. They'd been formed by a group of football enthusiasts from the Royal Arsenal munitions factory in Woolwich and charged sixpence for initial membership fees.

Suffice it to say that even in those heady south London days of 1886, 11 or so people paying sixpence didn't go very far. The team didn't actually have changing rooms until they moved to the Invicta Ground in 1890, so it's no great surprise that they had to get by with whatever gear they could beg, borrow or generally blag.

This included shirts. The team had been joined by a couple of former Nottingham Forest players who had moved to south London to work at the munitions factory. They still had links back to the Midlands club, so the people setting up Dial Square decided it was worth writing to the 'Tricky Trees' to see if they had any kits that they could spare. Forest very kindly obliged and, by some accounts, even sent something else that the chaps from the Dial Square team lacked: a ball.

Back in those days, Forest played in a dark, redcurrant shade of red, so that's what Arsenal played in for those first few decades. It was the shade that Arsenal returned to for the final season at Highbury in 2005/06.

★ CLIFF BASTIN ★

Cliff Bastin joined Arsenal from Exeter. Legendary Arsenal manager Herbert Chapman (see page 30) had gone to Vicarage Road one evening towards the end of the 1927/28 season to watch Watford play the West Country team. He had gone there to assess the performance of a promising Hornet, but was so impressed by Bastin's performance that the 17-year-old Grecian was signed for the Gunners instead.

What followed was a glittering career, with Bastin playing in teams that won the FA Cup in 1929/30 and 1935/36, the First Division five times in 1930/31, 1932/33, 1933/34, 1934/35 and 1937/38 and the FA Charity Shield five times in 1930, 1931, 1933, 1934 and 1938.

He became Arsenal's leading goal scorer, putting in 178 goals in all competitions between 1929 and 1947. His record stood until 1997, when Ian Wright took his crown and became Arsenal's top scorer, going on to score 185 goals. Wright was deposed, in turn, eight years later, by Thierry Henry, who ultimately scored 228.

Returning to Bastin ... He can be seen playing in the football sections of the classic 1939 film *The Arsenal Stadium Mystery*, which, as the name suggests, was a detective story based around Highbury that used footage from Arsenal's final game of the 1938/39 season.

His poor hearing (presumably caused by the cheering of the crowds at Highbury) meant that he was deemed not eligible for active service during World War II, contributing instead by working as an ARP warden at Highbury, which was used as an air raid shelter for the duration of hostilities.

After he retired, he eventually returned to the West Country to run the Horse & Groom pub in Exeter, but he'll always be remembered in north London for the way he drove a coach and horses through opposition defences. That joke would have been funny in the 1930s.

Something else that's funny is that Bastin only played for Exeter 17 times before heading off to London to seek fame and fortune. 17 times and there's still a stand named after him at St James Park where Exeter play. Makes you wonder what they'd have dedicated to him if he'd stayed in the West Country.

PACKING UP AND
★ HEADING NORTH ★

Woolwich Arsenal's second stint at the Manor Ground lasted around 20 years, and they extended the ground so that it could hold around 33,000 people on match days.

There was a problem, though. South London, at the time, was only just starting to grow, and the Manor Ground was relatively difficult to get to, so the team was only attracting around 11,000 spectators on a Saturday afternoon. By comparison, north of the river, Chelsea was said to be able to regularly command 28,000 people.

This isn't a question of 'my club's bigger than your club', it's a question of gate receipts. Football was a long way from becoming the global, multi-platform phenomenon that it is today, and gate receipts were a club's main source of income. If you are only getting around a quarter of the punters through the gate that your opposition is getting, you are less likely to be able to compete for players. It doesn't matter if you are paying them one shilling per week in the 1900s or £1 million an hour in the 2020s, if the other team is offering more, there's a chance that the player you want will sign for them.

Woolwich Arsenal were struggling both on the pitch and financially, and in 1913 they found themselves relegated. Incoming chairman Henry Norris needed to make a decision to either accept a future in football's lower divisions or do something radical.

He investigated the possibility of merging Woolwich Arsenal with Fulham, his other (spare) team, but, in the end, decided that the best thing he could do was move the team to north London, settling on the suburb of Highbury.

The club moved to their new home in 1913 and were warmly welcomed by the community and their new neighbours. They made the decision to drop the 'Woolwich' part of their name at around the same time, and moved forward with the streamlined 'Arsenal FC' as their moniker.

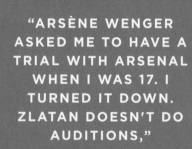

"ARSÈNE WENGER ASKED ME TO HAVE A TRIAL WITH ARSENAL WHEN I WAS 17. I TURNED IT DOWN. ZLATAN DOESN'T DO AUDITIONS,"

remembers Zlatan Ibrahimovic.

★ HERBERT CHAPMAN ★

Herbert Chapman's fingerprints are all over Arsenal. Almost any decision made about the team in the mid-1920s and early 1930s appears to have been signed off by him and, to this day, many of those decisions proved to be the right ones.

Changing the kits to red and white? Chapman. Putting floodlights on the redeveloped West Stand despite the opposition of the FA? Chapman. Lobbying to get the name of Gillespie Road underground station changed to Arsenal because everyone's heard of Arsenal and no one's heard of Gillespie Road? Chapman. Numbered shirts? Chapman.

He joined the club in 1925 and died while still in post in 1934, so all of these decisions, which hold up to this day, were made during a nine-year period that turned Arsenal's fortunes around. It is even said that he designed the Arsenal stadium's turnstiles and scoreboard, although it's difficult to work out where he found the time.

And this is before we've even got to the football.

In many ways, he was the game's first modern manager, analysing the requirements of the team and telling the board what they needed to buy rather than letting the board set the agenda. He enforced training regimes, hired physios and introduced new tactics and formations that enabled Arsenal to become the dominant team in the 1930s. His policy of holding friendly matches with teams in Europe enabled him to see how the game was evolving elsewhere and test his players in different situations.

Despite coming second in the League during Chapman's first season in charge (his former club Huddersfield came first, their third successive win), Arsenal endured a middling few years while Chapman refined his strategies and got the right people in the right places.

Then came 1930 and a 2–0 FA Cup victory against the then-mighty Huddersfield. This was followed by topping the First Division in 1930/31 and 1932/33, and bringing the FA Charity Shield to Highbury in 1930, 1931 and 1933. The backbone of the Arsenal team that he created at the start of the decade went on to win five First Division titles over the next 10 years. The fast, counter-attacking style of play that he refined defined Arsenal for a generation.

He loved football and ignored convention, signing Walter Tull, one of the first black professionals in Britain, to his Northampton side in 1911. He also attempted to bring

Austrian goalkeeper Rudy Hiden to Arsenal in 1930, although for once he didn't get his own way after protests from the Players' Union and the Football League led to the move being blocked by the Ministry of Labour.

He was, as they say, a man ahead of his time.

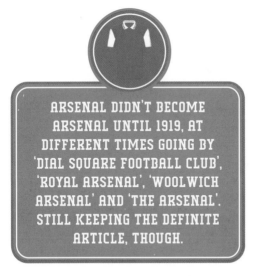

ARSENAL DIDN'T BECOME ARSENAL UNTIL 1919, AT DIFFERENT TIMES GOING BY 'DIAL SQUARE FOOTBALL CLUB', 'ROYAL ARSENAL', 'WOOLWICH ARSENAL' AND 'THE ARSENAL'. STILL KEEPING THE DEFINITE ARTICLE, THOUGH.

THE
★ ARSENAL STADIUM ★

Having made the decision to move from the Manor Ground, Arsenal looked at potential sites in Battersea and Harringay, but Highbury was, on balance, the best solution because the local tube station would make it easier to attract bigger crowds. And bigger crowds meant more gate money.

Henry Norris, chairman of both Arsenal and Fulham football clubs, mayor of Fulham and later MP for Fulham East, was an important character in the early years of Arsenal, and had an enviable network of contacts. If he was around today, he'd qualify for a blue tick on Twitter and have some sort of gold star next to his profile on LinkedIn (if that's their thing).

Among his contact list were several prominent members of the clergy. This is utterly irrelevant – and you should forget that it was ever mentioned.

By a strange coincidence, though, Norris was able to secure a 21-year lease on six acres of church land for a reasonable price slap-bang in the middle of Highbury, despite the opposition of both the neighbouring football team and local residents who didn't want the match-day disruption.

The deal went through, the final game at the Manor Ground was played in April 1913 and the first game at Arsenal Stadium kicked off at the start of September the same year, with 20,000 people turning up to witness a victory against Leicester Fosse.

Things in football never seem to quite roll in a straight line, particularly during the early days, but it's worth noting that the stadium at Highbury was officially always called the 'Arsenal Stadium', never 'Highbury', and the Arsenal London Underground station was originally called 'Gillespie Road', before being officially renamed in 1932. It is the only station on the Underground network to be named after a football team.

Norris' plans to get Arsenal up to the top flight (which had nothing to do with the fact that he had invested a considerable sum into creating the Arsenal Stadium) were put on hold by the outbreak of World War I.

★ TED DRAKE ★

Ted Drake joined Arsenal in 1934 from Southampton for the princely sum of £6,500. He is still the club's joint-fifth most prolific scorer, delivering 139 goals alongside Jimmy Brain. He enjoyed a long list of honours with his Arsenal teammates in the 1930s, winning the League in 1934/5.

He was a prolific goal scorer that season, scoring almost a goal a game (41 in 42 league matches). Unbelievably his three hat-tricks that season weren't his most impressive achievement, as he also managed to score four goals in one game – on four occasions.

On the way to winning the 1935/36 season, he tucked seven away at Aston Villa. It would have been eight, but the referee didn't agree that the goal he struck off the crossbar had gone over the line. It may have been that the ref just thought he was being greedy. Either way, it's a top-flight record that stands to this day. He also won the 1935/36 FA Cup and lifted the League trophy again in 1937/38.

He was one of seven Arsenal players that played for England against Italy in 1934, scoring the third goal in what was, by all accounts, a tetchy 3–2 win. He also turned out occasionally for the Hampshire County Cricket Club, because there's never much to do in the summer.

THE OPPOSITION: ★ TOTTENHAM ★

In 1913, Woolwich Arsenal were struggling financially because its ground was in a part of London that was difficult to get to. The decision to move from the Manor Ground to north London – just down the road from Tottenham – the year before the start of World War I is one reason why there is such a lot of tension between Tottenham and Arsenal, but the beef comes from several other incidents as well.

For example, Arsenal enjoyed promotion to the newly expanded First Division in 1919 while Tottenham found themselves relegated in an incident that, to modern eyes, might look like 'interesting circumstances' but – on balance – was probably just the normal cut and thrust of early 20th-century football (see page 44).

Arsenal have also been consistently the better team throughout the Premier League era, and some of the players that left White Hart Lane have been arguably a little bit less than complimentary about their former employers when they have turned up at Highbury.

It could be said that where Arsenal loses the moral high ground is when it comes to the race issue, which has led to embarrassing scenes by a minority of fans that the club has had to denounce several times after north London derbies.

These are the main reasons why there is tension between Arsenal and Tottenham fans, which has almost guaranteed that north London derbies will be occasions to relish until the eventual heat death of the universe.

Looking at the numbers for the Premier League up to the end of the 2021/22 season, Arsenal beat their north

London rivals 37% of the time and drew 37% of the time, meaning that they let Tottenham have the bragging rights around 25% of the time. Drilling down into it a bit, Arsenal win at home just under 60% of the time, but have only won at White Hart Lane or the Tottenham Stadium around 16% of the time, so cherish every away win.

If football is entertainment, though, the most important statistic is that Premier League matches between Arsenal and Tottenham only end in a 0-0 result 8% of the time, compared to 10% against Chelsea and 11% against Manchester United. Whatever the reason for the distaste between the two teams, there's a decent chance they will deliver goals.

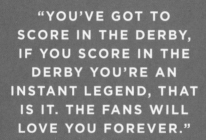

"YOU'VE GOT TO SCORE IN THE DERBY, IF YOU SCORE IN THE DERBY YOU'RE AN INSTANT LEGEND, THAT IS IT. THE FANS WILL LOVE YOU FOREVER."

David Rocastle offers some helpful advice to Ian Wright ahead of the north London derby.

★ REG LEWIS ★

Reg Lewis spent his entire 18-year career as a professional footballer with Arsenal. If it hadn't been for losing a third of that time to World War II, there's a decent chance that he would be considerably higher than 12th in the pantheon of all-time Arsenal goal scorers.

He scored 143 goals in 130 appearances for Arsenal during the six years of conflict, but these weren't official games so the goals don't count. If the League had been running and he'd only scored half that number against professional teams rather than teams that were pulled together, he'd be comfortably within sight of 200 goals. If ifs and buts were pots and pans …

Lewis was Arsenal's top scorer in 1946/47, scoring 29 goals, and he formed a successful partnership with Ronnie Rooke for the 1947/48 season that delivered 47 goals and the First Division title. He helped Arsenal win the Charity Shield in 1948, as well as the FA Cup in 1950. Injuries forced him to retire in 1953 and he went on to run a pub and work in insurance.

REGARDING THE
★ EVENTS OF 1919 ★

As we might have mentioned, there is not a lot of love lost between Arsenal and Tottenham. There are many reasons for this – some of it the fault of the folks in white, some of it the folks in red – but it is Arsenal, potentially unfairly, that have been accused of the original sin. Let's try to shed a bit of light on the 1919 incident.

In 1919, as everything started to get back to some semblance of normal after the horrors of World War I, a decision was made by the English FA to extend the First Division from 20 to 22 clubs. Simple enough, although there was a slight complication in that the relegations and promotions had to be based on the conclusion of the 1914/15 season, because no one had played professionally during the hostilities.

The plan was for the top two teams from the Second Division in 1914/15, Derby County and Preston North End, to enjoy automatic promotion, and the bottom two teams in the First Division, Tottenham and Chelsea, to be relegated as normal. There would then be a vote to decide which two Second Division teams would be invited to play in the top division for the 1919/20 season.

Concentrate, because this is where it gets complicated.

For context, Tottenham had come last in the 1914/15 season. Only by a point, but last nonetheless. Arsenal, meanwhile, had finished fifth in the Second Division. They were seven points behind the team that was promoted in second place. But every team in the Second Division was invited to put themselves forward for promotion before all the clubs voted on who would be elevated.

These sorts of things are always complicated, and the historical records are deeply fuzzy, but what seems to have happened is that Chelsea, who were second from bottom of the First Division at the end of the season five years before, received a unanimous vote to come straight back into the newly extended First Division. This was because, fascinatingly and very much allegedly, third-from-bottom Manchester United is said to have fixed a game against Liverpool so they ended the season a point above Chelsea and just clear of the drop zone. Allegedly.

Two teams being relegated meant that there were four positions available in the First Division. Derby County, Preston North End and Chelsea took the first three berths. There was one more place in the First Division to be decided by vote.

The bare facts are that Tottenham had every right to stand for election back to the First Division, but Arsenal and several others also proposed themselves for promotion. This included Nottingham Forest, who incidentally finished third from bottom in the Second Division and still tried to argue that they deserved a place in the top flight.

When it came to the vote, Arsenal received 18 votes and Tottenham eight, Barnsley five, Wolves four, Nottingham Forest three and Birmingham two. Hull received a single vote, presumably because you can always count on yourself for a nomination.

Since that day, there have been accusations of grubby back-room deals and electoral shenanigans. Fingers have been wagged in the direction of Arsenal chairman the Right Honourable Henry Norris MP, who was also both chairman and mayor of Fulham at the time. It has been suggested that he had used his considerable influence to get Arsenal into the top tier at the expense of Tottenham. There is no actual evidence that this was the case, but in the interests of fairness it should probably be mentioned that he was later removed from his position with Arsenal and banned from all footballing activities for impropriety in the mid-1920s for, among other things, offering players extra financial inducements to join Arsenal, and pocketing the proceeds from the sale of the team bus. Yes, really.

We are unlikely to ever really know what happened, but it's worth pointing out that it was over a century ago, and that Tottenham bounced straight back into the First Division as champions the next season. Maybe it's time to move on. We know a guy that can sort you out a decent deal on a team bus if you need transport.

"IF WENGER HAD STRENGTHENED IN THE WINDOW, ARSENAL COULD HAVE BEEN STRONGER,"

says Tony Cascarino, showing why his football analysis is so much in demand.

"ARSENAL'S WIDTH COMES FROM WIDE AREAS."

Jamie Redknapp offers some truly deep insight into the game of football.

★ BOB WILSON ★

Bob Wilson has been involved with Arsenal for well over half a century, and has helped the team win three doubles during that time. The first was as goalie in the 1970/71 season when he played in every league and cup match, with the team conceding the second fewest goals in the League that season.

His strategy of diving at opposition attackers' feet led to him suffering more than his fair share of injuries, and so he retired relatively early for a goalie at 32. At that point, in addition to his extensive media work, Wilson also became a mainstay of the Arsenal goalkeeper coaching team. He spent 28 years as goalkeeping coach, helping Pat Jennings, John Lukic and David Seaman hone their skills, playing an active role in two more Arsenal double-winning seasons in the process.

Wilson started his career as a professional player relatively late, with his father persuading him to train as a teacher rather than sign for Manchester United in his youth. It was probably because he wanted to make sure that his son had a career to fall back on.

ST TOTTERINGHAM'S
★ DAY ★

Tottenham's fans celebrate St Hotspur Day on 14th April, the anniversary of two matches when they managed to overcome the odds and beat Arsenal. The first was in 1991 in the FA Cup, when, credit where credit's due, Paul Gascoigne scored a sublime goal and Gary Lineker scored another couple. The other was in 2010. It happens. Good for them; it's important to look back in the history books and find things to shout about.

Since the start of the 21st century, though, Arsenal have taken to celebrating something far more entertaining. There is a day in most football seasons when it becomes mathematically impossible for Tottenham to beat Arsenal. That day is St Totteringham's Day – named in honour of a doddering and completely made-up saint of north London.

The nice thing about St Totteringham's Day is that it's a movable feast – and it gives an exceptional indicator of how a season is going. Some seasons it is celebrated on the last day of the season, sometimes it's in late April, but it has been celebrated as early as 9th March (in 2008, when the tipping point was reached with nine games remaining). It has also been celebrated with 10 games remaining during the year of the 'Invincibles', you'll be astonished to hear, but vagaries of the football fixtures meant that that wasn't until 13th March. It was celebrated for 21 consecutive years between the 1995/96 and the 2015/16 seasons.

To be fair to Tottenham, they have been improving in recent seasons, and St Totteringham's Day has become less of a regular occurrence than it was. It fell on April 21 in the 2022/23 season though, which is nice.

ARSENAL AND INNOVATION: ⭐ RADIO HAMS ⭐

Football and technology have a funny relationship. There has always been a focus on making sure that, as far as possible, the game played in the Premier League by multimillionaire show ponies is the same as the one that's played down at the rec on a Saturday afternoon by a bunch of hoofers with jumpers for goalposts.

When there's a trophy, a Champions League place or a potential relegation at stake, then there's a little more pressure to get things right (important though the post-kickabout bragging rights are), and so technology has played an increasingly important role in the professional game. If only to stop people moaning about dodgy offside decisions – because VAR's done away with controversy, which is great.

But away from the mechanics of the game itself,

technology has also played a role in how spectators take a match in, and Arsenal has always been among the first teams to be involved.

In January 1927, Arsenal hosted Sheffield United, as well as the BBC's commentators and microphones – the first time that a football match had enjoyed live commentary. The team describing events devised a scheme for helping listeners understand where the action was taking place; they divided the pitch into eight sections. It should be pointed out that while the game between Arsenal and Sheffield United was the first association football match to be broadcast on the BBC, Wakelam and Lewis had taken the same approach to a Rugby Union game between England and Wales at Twickenham a week before. There's always a caveat.

So, what you ended up with was a commentator – the stupendously named Henry Blythe Thornhill 'Teddy' Wakelam – in his very best plummy interwar English accent providing an explanation of what was happening on the pitch while his partner shouted the sector number over the top of him. Chuck D and Flavor Flav made a similar approach work very well for Public Enemy, but it wasn't massively helpful for football commentaries. The microphones stayed, the numbers man went back to bingo. (This is not strictly true; the numbers man was C.A. Lewis, World War I fighter ace, one of the founding fathers of the BBC and, seemingly, an all-round fascinating chap.)

Although this form of commentary was phased out, fascinatingly it could be that the phrase 'back to square one' (used to describe a situation where someone is forced to go back to the start of a process), stems from this style of football commentary.

Either way, the radio broadcast was a success and by 1931, the BBC was broadcasting more than 100 games per season. The problem was that this success came at the same time as the economic downturn that followed the 1929 Wall Street Crash. The FA, alongside chairmen at various football clubs, thought that part of the reason for their dwindling revenues was the radio coverage, so broadcasters found themselves uninvited to stadiums on a Saturday afternoon until well after World War II.

"THE FIRST MAN IN A TACKLE NEVER GETS HURT."

Wilf Copping, defender in the 1930s, explains his approach to football in what was, by all accounts, a more civilised time.

★ PAT RICE ★

It takes a lot of people doing lots of different things to make a football club, and Pat Rice has done a lot of things for the club since he joined as an apprentice in 1964. During his first few years he only made occasional appearances, understudying at right back for bigger names, but when his chance came, he grabbed it, and by the 1970/71 double-winning season he was a mainstay of the team.

He became club captain in 1977, leading the team to victory over Manchester United in the 1979 FA Cup (and leading Arsenal to the finals in 1978 and 1980). He also earned 49 international caps playing for Northern Ireland.

He left Arsenal in 1980, joining Watford and helping them gain promotion to the First Division in 1981/82, and playing a role in getting them to the FA Cup final in 1984.

At the end of his playing days, he returned to Arsenal as a youth team coach, helping the team win the FA Youth Cup twice, and taking on the caretaker manager role shortly before the arrival of Arsène Wenger. He then became Wenger's assistant for 12 years, supporting the team to two doubles, the 'Invincibles' season and a trophy cabinet of other honours.

ARSENAL AND INNOVATION: THE ★ NUMBERS RACKET ★

A year after the first radio broadcast, Arsenal became one of the first two teams in England's top flight to play a match with numbers on their shirts. Playing against Sheffield Wednesday in August 1928, the decision to try out numbering the players was intended to help referees manage the game, with one team wearing shirts 1–11 and the other wearing 12–22 (this was in the days before substitutions).

The experiment was deemed a success, although Arsenal lost the match, with the Owls winning 3–2.

It is worth pointing out that Chelsea and Swansea experimented with numbered shirts on the same day as Arsenal and Sheffield Wednesday, although in the Arsenal game they only numbered the outfield players, not the goalies. They were in the Second Division at the time, though, so no one really noticed.

The Football League were swift to notice the benefits of having players in numbered shirts and leapt into action to support the innovation. A mere 11 years later, a rule was put in place that mandated numbered shirts for all games.

The reason for the delay was that leadership teams at several clubs thought numbering of players was an unnecessary affectation that made football players look like jockeys.

Numbering has become more nuanced as the years have gone by, with certain numbers being associated with certain positions or even certain players. For example, Ian Wright has always been associated with the number 8 shirt, which has also been worn by Freddie Ljungberg, Samir Nasri, Mikel Arteta, Aaron Ramsey and Martin Ødegaard. Some teams have a particular shirt that is strongly associated with a single player. Given the astonishing array of talent that has played for the Gunners over the years, as soon as one legend gives up the shirt, another tends to arise to take their place.

THE OPPOSITION: ★ CHELSEA ★

With Chelsea it tends to be the little things: the meetings with Ashley Cole; the 6-0 defeat that marred Wenger's 1,000th game in charge. Little things that add up.

The proximity of the two teams meant that their first meeting at Stamford Bridge in 1907 brought together

65,000 people, and still whenever the two teams meet they are guaranteed to draw a crowd – but the rivalry isn't particularly deep-seated. It's more like two people trying to get through the same door on a tube train: most of the time, one waits for the other and they both get to where they want to be without a hitch; sometimes, though, one will get in the way of the other and it can get a little alpha male. Everyone else rolls their eyes.

In terms of the statistics, the two teams have only really been in the ascendancy at the same time in recent years, which is reflected by the fact Arsenal have won around 40% of matches between the two teams since the start of the Premier League. If you narrow it down to pre- and post-2003 up to the 2022/23 season, before the Abramovich takeover in June 2003, Arsenal won over half of Premier League matches against Chelsea, but after the takeover that figure dropped to around a third.

In terms of goals, you get nearly two and three quarters goals per game on average during a Premier League meeting between the two, and you get four or more goals nearly a third of the time, so you've a decent chance of excitement. You've also got a 10% chance of a 0-0 draw though, but at least it's not far to get home after it's all over.

MANAGING MANAGERS
★ BETTER ★

It's a funny old thing, but when you look at it, Arsenal have only had 20 full-time managers since 1897 (discounting caretakers). That's a remarkable level of consistency given that, to pick a team at random, Spurs have had 21 managers since 1997. Obviously, there are several factors to take into account within that, not least of which is the remarkable Arsenal careers of George Morell (a seven-year tenure as manager), Leslie Knighton (six years), Herbert Chapman (nine years), George Allison (13 years), Tom Whittaker (nine years), Bertie Mee (10 years), Terry Neil (seven years), George Graham (nine years) and Arsène Wenger (22 years).

In the cut-throat world of football management, where managers tend to be given two transfer windows to get their squads in shape – if they are lucky – Arsenal's tendency to pick a direction and stick with it is probably part of the reason that the club inspires such loyalty and has won so many trophies down the years.

All this said, and not looking to downplay the importance of solid leadership on the pitch and in the dugout, it is also worth pointing out that Arsenal won the League in three consecutive seasons with three different managers, specifically Herbert Chapman in 1932/33, Joe Shaw in 1933/34 and George Allison in 1934/35. Part of this success may have been the result of Herbert Chapman's untimely death in the middle of the 1933/34 season, which presumably led the team to play up; and part of it may be that if you look at football statistics for long enough, you are always going to find the exception that proves the rule.

Either way, there are many things that need to go the right way if you are going to win a major tournament. Having a consistent team leadership that is supported by an understanding board, and having a team and fanbase that gets behind them are not everything – but they are a lot.

Looking specifically at the Premier League, Arsenal have had eight managers, four of which were caretakers. Even taking these caretakers into account, on average, these eight have spent four years in post, which is more than twice the time that managers of either Chelsea or Tottenham enjoy (which is around 19 months on average). This also does not take into account the six years that George Graham was in post before the dawn of the Premier League, when history truly started.

No matter how you look at it, Arsenal's commitment to its managers has been exceptional, even if you were to overlook Wenger's phenomenal contribution to the club.

MANAGERS DURING THE
★ PREMIER LEAGUE ERA ★

Manager	Joined	Left
George Graham	May 1986	February 1995
Stewart Houston (caretaker)	February 1995	June 1995
Bruce Rioch	June 1995	August 1996
Stewart Houston (caretaker)	August 1996	September 1996
Pat Rice (caretaker)	September 1996	September 1996
Arsène Wenger	October 1996	May 2018
Unai Emery	May 2018	November 2019
Freddie Ljungberg (caretaker)	November 2019	December 2019
Mikel Arteta	December 2019	Present

★ ALAN BALL ★

Alan Ball was the youngest of England's 1966 World Cup-winning squad, and was still in his prime when he signed for Arsenal in 1971 for what was then a record transfer fee. He'd also broken the English transfer fee record when he'd signed for Everton five years earlier. Arsenal were in a rebuilding phase when he arrived at Highbury, so while he was a major draw, the team itself could not repeat the success of the 1970/71 double. He became club captain in 1974.

In all, he made 217 appearances for the Gunners, providing 52 goals. He moved on mid-way though the 1976/77 season, playing for another good few years before going into management.

In the drab world of 1970s football, where you could wear boots in any colour so long as they were black or brown, Ball was famous for sporting white boots. Some might have said that was showy, but frankly, if you've got it, flaunt it.

A FOND FAREWELL TO
★ HIGHBURY ★

There came a point when Arsenal had to move on from Highbury, the scene of so many triumphs and mercifully few heartbreaks. The financial aspect wasn't the only factor; the existing ground was initially built in 1913 and had been rebuilt, patched and enhanced as far as it could be without encroaching on neighbouring homes and businesses, and the infrastructure around the stadium had been built in a different age.

During its final years, practical restrictions and all-seater stadiums meant that Highbury could only host around 40,000 fans, compared to just under 75,000 that fellow title contenders Manchester United could welcome to Old Trafford.

At the time that the decision to move on from Highbury was made, the Gunners had just delivered an impossible feat: going an entire season without being defeated.

Without banging on about that too much – because talking about it tends to make other clubs jealous – interest in the club was at an all-time high, and there was massive demand for tickets. The club faced a choice: they could put up prices to make sure that it could afford to keep attracting the talent that fans expected to see on the pitch, or they could rebuild bigger elsewhere so that they could get more people in through the gates.

Also, by this point some of the parts of Highbury had become so culturally significant they had been granted listed status, and it would have been very difficult to build around them to marry the needs of historical preservation with a modern stadium experience. Regulatory expectations had also changed beyond recognition and so, sadly, it was time to move.

Arsenal played their final game at the Arsenal Stadium at the end of the 2005/06 season, a memorable 4–2 victory over Wigan that clinched their Champions League place at the expense of Tottenham and, fittingly, included a Thierry Henry hat-trick.

The site of Highbury was redeveloped into housing that protects the building's listed features.

★ ARSENAL WOMEN ★

Arsenal Women was founded in 1987, romping to a stunning 33 trophies in its first 22 seasons under founding manager Vic Akers. Turning semi-professional in 2002, the teams that he developed won the FA Women's Cup 11 times, the FA Women's Premier League Cup 10 times and the FA Women's Premier League 11 times.

As part of this, they enjoyed five Premier League/FA Women's Cup doubles as well as four domestic trebles. They were also the first English team to win the UEFA Women's Cup in 2007. Which is not a bad start.

In total, Arsenal Women FC has won the top flight of the women's game 15 times, the FA Cup 14 times, the League Cup six times, the League Cup 10 times, the Community Shield five times (once shared), and the Women's Champions League once.

Playing out of Borehamwood, Arsenal have worked hard to ensure that the women's team receives the same attention as the men's, and the team have repaid the support with a string of legendary performances, including an unbeaten run of 108 games without defeat that lasted from 2003 to 2009.

Arsenal's women's team was one of the founder members of the FA Women's Super League in 2011, winning the first two seasons.

Competition in women's football has been increasing over the last decade with several other teams getting in on the act and bringing through talented footballers – a fact that played a significant role in England's Lionesses winning the Euros in 2022. At the same time, it also meant that Arsenal no longer had an assumed right to write its name on every cup or trophy they competed for. Honours have been less frequent as a result, but the quality of the competition has driven the players to new heights, and the Arsenal team continue to challenge in both the domestic and the European leagues.

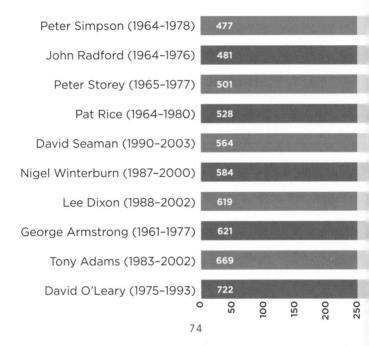

Peter Simpson (1964–1978) 477
John Radford (1964–1976) 481
Peter Storey (1965–1977) 501
Pat Rice (1964–1980) 528
David Seaman (1990–2003) 564
Nigel Winterburn (1987–2000) 584
Lee Dixon (1988–2002) 619
George Armstrong (1961–1977) 621
Tony Adams (1983–2002) 669
David O'Leary (1975–1993) 722

0 50 100 150 200 250

ARSENAL'S TOP TEN FIRST TEAM
★ APPEARANCES ★

(ALL COMPETITIONS)

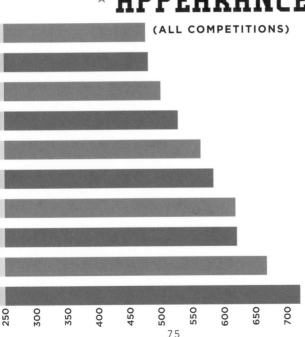

250   300   350   400   450   500   550   600   650   700   750

★ PAT JENNINGS ★

There are many ways of getting one over on your neighbours, one of which is taking one of their players (one that they think is near the end of their career), welcoming them in and getting another eight years of first team football out of them.

This is basically what happened with Pat Jennings, who spent 13 years with Tottenham, making 590 appearances in all competitions, for them, and then moved to Highbury and held on to the number 1 shirt for the best part of a decade, helping Arsenal lift the FA Cup in 1979 and be runners-up in in 1978 and 1980, and come second in the 1980 final of the European Cup Winners' Cup. Second place is just first loser, but it's an impressive run nonetheless.

In 1983, he became the first player to make 1,000 first team appearances in top-flight English football, and in 1986, at 41, he became the oldest player to turn out for a World Cup. He was playing for Northern Ireland and the opponents were Brazil, so at least he had a busy swansong.

ARSENAL AND
★ CONTROVERSY ★

Arsenal and its precursors have often courted controversy, basically because the team has never been willing to settle for being simply another team.

One of the first times this happened was when Woolwich Arsenal had the audacity to turn professional and pay the players for the entertainment they provided. This scandalised Victorian south London, several local teams refused to play the team and they were kicked out of the London Football Association.

The team carried on regardless and proceeded to bring home several trophies as the 19th century gave way to the 20th.

A little over a hundred years later, Arsenal had the audacity to bring in Arsène Wenger as manager, making the Frenchman the first foreign manager to manage a team in what was then the Premiership. This scandalised the whole of the footballing community across England for some reason, possibly because they felt that someone without a blue passport would struggle to understand the nuances of the sacred English game.

The team carried on regardless and proceeded to bring home more than several trophies as the 20th century gave way to the 21st.

It's not just in the fields of professionalism and football management where Arsenal have challenged conventions. In the 1930s, Herbert Chapman had floodlights fitted on to the newly constructed West Stand at the Arsenal Stadium, but the Football League refused to let them be used, presumably assuming that they were powered by witchcraft or some such. It seems that the Football Association only relented two decades later when the teams that had them installed (which, by this point, was pretty much all of them) used them for some friendly matches – which proved the value of being able to play some matches in the evening.

Even the clock at the Clock End caused raised eyebrows when it was put up. It initially counted the 45-minute halves of a match (this was in the days before Fergie time was a thing) so spectators and players could see how long was left. The FA didn't like this – they felt that it undermined the match officials who are, of course, the ultimate arbiters of time – and Arsenal were forced to put up a more traditional clock.

At its best, Arsenal doesn't talk about daring to do, it simply does. The team's leadership will take a risk to do what it thinks is right, irrespective of what the prevailing culture says at the time. It's probably fair to say that most of the time it turns out fine. On balance.

"I WILL SIGN EVERY CONTRACT ARSENAL PUT IN FRONT OF ME WITHOUT READING IT."

Tony Adams' accountant is probably glad he never had to try to negotiate with Herbert Chapman.

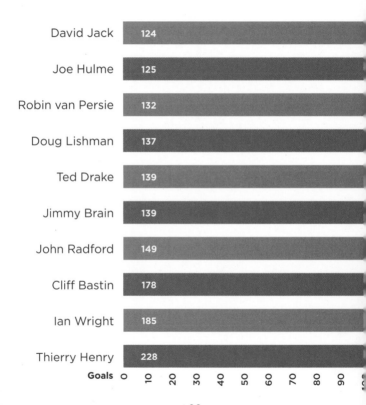

	Goals
David Jack	124
Joe Hulme	125
Robin van Persie	132
Doug Lishman	137
Ted Drake	139
Jimmy Brain	139
John Radford	149
Cliff Bastin	178
Ian Wright	185
Thierry Henry	228

ARESENAL'S LEADING ALL-TIME ★ GOAL SCORERS ★

(ALL COMPETITIONS)

110 120 130 140 150 160 170 180 190 200 210 220 230 240

★ TONY ADAMS ★

Tony Adams is a legend in a club full of legends. He pulled on the Arsenal shirt 669 times and spent his entire 19-year playing career at Highbury, winning four top-flight titles across three decades. He became Arsenal captain in 1988, retaining the role for 14 years.

He also won 66 England caps, many of them as captain, and played at four major tournaments.

In many ways there were two distinct phases to his career. In the first phase, he formed an indomitable defensive partnership with Steve Bould, Lee Dixon and Nigel Winterburn, giving Arsenal teams of the 1980s and early 1990s a solid foundation on which to build their attacks.

The arrival of Arsène Wenger brought an evolution in footballing style and Adams adapted his football to fit right in. While he may have lacked pace, his strength and understanding of the game made his regular runs forward with the ball out of defence a key part of the successful Arsenal teams of the late 1990s and early 2000s.

As winner of the First Division and Premier League in 1988/89, 1990/91, 1997/98 and 2001/02, the FA Cup in 1992/93, 1997/98 and 2001/02, the Football League Cup in 1986/87 and 1992/93, the Football League Centenary

Trophy in 1988, the FA Charity Shield in 1991 and 1998 and the European Cup Winners' Cup in 1993/94 , they call him 'Mr Arsenal'. Rightly so. Just don't let him take you dancing.

THE GUNNERS HOLD THE RECORD FOR THE MOST CONSECUTIVE CLEAN SHEETS IN THE CHAMPIONS LEAGUE. MAKING THEIR WAY TO THE FINAL IN 2006, THEY MANAGED 10 STRAIGHT CLEAN SHEETS. JENS LEHMANN WAS RESPONSIBLE FOR NINE OF THEM. IT'S AN IMPRESSIVE RECORD, BUT YOU'D SUSPECT THEY WOULD RATHER HAVE WON THE FINAL INSTEAD OF LOSING 2-1 TO BARCELONA.

"PLAY FOR THE NAME ON THE FRONT OF THE SHIRT, AND THEY WILL REMEMBER THE NAME ON THE BACK."

Tony Adams

★ EMIRATES RISES ★

After several years of planning, the Emirates Stadium opened its doors to competitive football in 2006, ushering in a new era for Arsenal. The new stadium has tried to subtly emulate some of the features of Highbury, with the pitch running north–south and player tunnels and dug outs running down the west side.

While Highbury could host 38,000 people, Emirates offered upwards of 61,000 seats. While it would be nice to live in a world where money is not a consideration and there's a constant stream of phenomenal new talent being nurtured through the ranks of the youth team, the reality is that money is a major consideration for any team that wants to compete at the highest level.

Arsenal focused on funding the development of the Emirates on a financially sound basis. This meant that for several years the club was forced to allow players to move on quickly, and the team perhaps lacked the final flourish that is needed to win the League or compete for the trophies. It was a frustrating period, but it was necessary to make sure that they were on a sound financial footing.

It has been estimated that the club's match-day revenue from the Emirates' executive boxes and 'Club Level', where you get posh seats and canapés, is almost equivalent to the revenue from the whole Highbury stadium, which puts the team in a good place to build upon – and perhaps return to – past glories in a new setting. The evidence of the 2022/23 season certainly seems to be pointing in that direction.

In 2009, there was a move to ensure what is called the 'Arsenalisation' of the stadium, with more statues of Arsenal legends erected, more iconography and the reintroduction of the Clock End, featuring a replica of the original Highbury clock, beefed up to reflect its enhanced environment (the original clock can still be seen perched happily on the outside of the Emirates Stadium).

The annoying thing about time, though, is that it's already more than 16 years since Arsenal moved to the Emirates – the naming sponsorship has been extended and they are starting to talk about refurbishment, because some of the technology is now obsolete (and the neighbours down the road may have got something bigger and shinier). Nothing ever stands still.

THE OPPOSITION: ★ MANCHESTER CITY ★

Someone once said that football is a 'funny old game', and it seems likely that they were right. If you look at the relationship between Arsenal and Manchester City, they have never been in the ascendancy at the same time, until recently (hopefully).

The clubs' antecedents first met in 1894 in the old Second Division, playing each other regularly as they became established. Manchester City were promoted to the First Division as Second Division champions in 1902/03, six points ahead of Woolwich Arsenal, who were promoted a year later.

From there, they've met most years in one form or another, with Arsenal taking home the honours most of the time. There has been something of a change in recent years – no one's really sure why – but, whatever the reason, there's not much point looking into the stats.

Arsenal ran them close in the 2022/23 season, but it's difficult to argue with the fact that Manchester City assembled an exceptional team with a phenomenal manager. If winning the Premier League was easy, then everyone would be doing it, and the fact that Arsenal came close is pretty satisfying. Just not quite as satisfying as winning the trophy …

IN 1893, ARSENAL BECAME THE FIRST SOUTHERN CLUB TO JOIN THE FOOTBALL LEAGUE.

★ LEE DIXON ★

Lee Dixon was playing in defence for Stoke City when Arsenal beat them 3-0 in the FA Cup in 1987, but Gunners' manager George Graham clearly saw something he wanted for his team and first signed Dixon, and then his defensive partner Steve Bould, shortly afterwards.

Dixon was a regular part of the Arsenal squad for the next 15 years, holding his position and adapting his game to suit Arsène Wenger's strategies. He played for Arsenal 619 times in all competitions, winning the First Division in 1988/89 and 1990/91, the Premier League in 1997/98 and 2001/02, the FA Cup three times, the FA Charity Shield three times and the European Cup Winners' Cup once – quite a haul. It would seem his superstitious insistence to always go out onto the pitch third – after David Seaman and Tony Adams – has worked wonders.

He was called up for England 22 times, a number that would have been higher if he hadn't suffered badly timed injuries and if England had actually got around to qualifying for the 1994 World Cup.

ARSENAL AND INNOVATION: VIDEO DID WHAT TO THE ★ RADIO STAR? ★

The Gunners took their televisual bow just over a decade after they'd been one of the first teams to play in a match broadcast on the radio. A match between Arsenal and Arsenal Reserves was screened from the Arsenal Stadium in September 1937. Mobile phones and satellites mean we can now have a video call with someone virtually anywhere in the world, so it's hard to imagine the technical feat that televised football represented 80 years ago. At the time, the TV cameras were about the size of an average family car but were significantly less manoeuvrable, and the stadiums didn't have the infrastructure to support them.

As a result, logistics, costs and a fear that televising matches would reduce gate receipts essentially kept television out of football for a couple of decades. The reasons why Arsenal were involved in the first radio and television broadcasts aren't hard to fathom, though. Highbury is located near to the Alexandra Palace broadcasting transmitter, so it would have been relatively simple to get the cameras to the stadium and the broadcasts out to the world.

Arsenal were also involved in the first football match to be broadcast in 3D in 2010. The technology hasn't really taken off, but there were nearly 30 years between the first match being shown on the TV and regular TV highlights shows, so it might be more of a thing by the mid-2040s.

What seems more likely, though, is that Arsenal will be one of the first teams to be involved in a live football match in the metaverse, with players live-scanned into a Minecraft or Fortnite environment and fans able to decide whether their personal background for the match will be the Emirates, Highbury, the Manor Ground or even simply an unspecified field on the Isle of Dogs. Because that's progress.

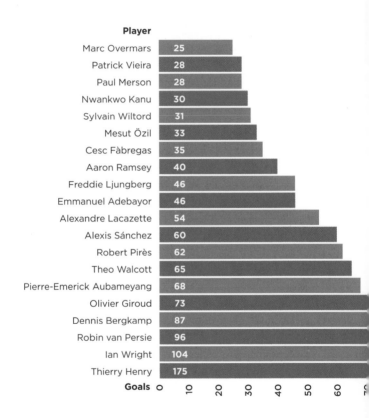

Player	Goals
Marc Overmars	25
Patrick Vieira	28
Paul Merson	28
Nwankwo Kanu	30
Sylvain Wiltord	31
Mesut Özil	33
Cesc Fàbregas	35
Aaron Ramsey	40
Freddie Ljungberg	46
Emmanuel Adebayor	46
Alexandre Lacazette	54
Alexis Sánchez	60
Robert Pirès	62
Theo Walcott	65
Pierre-Emerick Aubameyang	68
Olivier Giroud	73
Dennis Bergkamp	87
Robin van Persie	96
Ian Wright	104
Thierry Henry	175

ARSENAL'S LEADING PREMIER LEAGUE ★ GOAL SCORERS ★

WENGER VERSUS FERGUSON: THE CLASH THAT SHAPED THE ★ PREMIER LEAGUE ★

United were the ultimate team in the 1990s, but Arsenal were the upcoming team. Once Wenger had ascended the throne at Highbury, the needle with Sir Alex Ferguson – the young pretender versus the old master – very quickly and visibly became clear.

There is an argument that the rivalry with Ferguson helped Wenger establish himself as a manager and a leader at a club where his arrival had been broadly greeted with a collective "Who?" Wenger made it clear pretty early on that it was his mission to challenge United for Premier League dominance. It's fair to say that he achieved that ambition for a while back there.

It got very spicy indeed, with matches between the two teams regularly being punctuated by brawls on the pitch and handbags in the tunnel post-match. The pantomime became a twice-seasonal highlight, but, to be honest, it started to eclipse the sublime football on the pitch that both teams were capable of producing.

Just as both managers were starting to recognise that their rivalry might be getting in the way of the football, Roman Abramovich manifested over Stamford Bridge, changing the dynamic in the Premier League and bringing José Mourinho's pithy turns of phrase – which quickly attracted a healthy proportion of Wenger and Ferguson's ire. It certainly helped the Manchester United and Arsenal managers come to something of a détente in their latter years. From the sound of things, the pair enjoy a fairly cordial relationship now that they have stepped back from the front line of football.

★ IAN WRIGHT ★

Some footballers manage to burst on to the scene at 16, coming off the bench in the 70th minute to breathless commentary after their exploits in the German league or with the England Under-21s, making their inclusion a foregone conclusion. Some take their time over it, having promising spells on loan with League Two clubs and then stepping up when an injury crisis looms.

Some very nearly give up on their dreams of becoming a professional footballer and work as a bricklayer before being spotted playing Sunday league and being invited for a trial at Crystal Palace, acing it, going on to become a mainstay of their first team before signing for Arsenal six years later, and becoming their top scorer six years in a row. These players raise the FA Cup twice (1992/93 and 1997/98), win the Football League Cup (in 1992/93), the European Cup Winners' Cup (1993/94), and wash it all down with a Premier League title (1997/98). And get caught roller-blading down the historically significant marble halls of Highbury. And become a bona fide legend.

To be fair, there's only one player that's done that. It's Ian Wright. As you probably already guessed.

THE OPPOSITION: ★ MANCHESTER UNITED

Games against Manchester United really used to mean something. When title hopes or cup runs were put to the sword by a trip to Old Trafford or Highbury. When Arsenal were the only thing that stood in the way of Manchester United's dominance, and Manchester United were the only thing that stood in the way of Arsenal's.

It is tempting to think that the rivalry between the clubs only really kicked into gear in the mid-1990s when Arsenal started to challenge regularly for the title, but the reality is a little more nuanced. Relations between the two clubs had been getting gradually more and more acerbic since the mid-1980s.

In the final season of the old First Division, both Arsenal and Manchester United were docked points after a brawl involving 21 players, although according to the match commentators most of those were trying to calm things down. Arsenal were deducted two points as a result of the melee, although this didn't stop them from going on to top the table, seven points clear of Liverpool and 24 points clear of sixth-placed Manchester United.

In many ways, that set the tone for the next two decades of games between the two teams as they both strove to bring in trophies and league titles. However, clashes between the two have been more subdued in recent years as both have gone through extensive rebuilding periods with some relatively fallow seasons as a result. It is probably a rivalry that is just waiting to resurface if the teams manage to recapture the eminence of their glory days, though.

Rather than focus on the history of the teams' brawls, though, let's have a look at how their statistics stack up during the Premier League era. Between the 1992/93 and 2022/23 seasons, Arsenal have won 29% of their games against Manchester United and drawn exactly the same proportion. Best not ask what they did with the remaining 42% ... Playing at either the Arsenal Stadium or the Emirates, Arsenal have won 45% of matches, but victories at Old Trafford have been scant, with Arsenal only winning 13% of the time.

On a brighter note, the two teams have, on average, provided 2.5 goals per Premier League meeting, with only 11% of matches deflating to 0-0, so it's a potentially great match if you are looking for entertainment.

IN AUGUST 2011, THE GUNNERS HAD THEIR WORST EVER LEAGUE DEFEAT, WHEN THEY WERE BEATEN 8-2 BY MANCHESTER UNITED AT OLD TRAFFORD.

FERGUSON ON WENGER, AND WENGER ON ★ FERGUSON ★

"HE HAS NO EXPERIENCE OF ENGLISH FOOTBALL. HE HAS COME HERE FROM JAPAN, AND NOW HE IS TELLING EVERYONE HOW TO ORGANISE OUR FOOTBALL. UNLESS YOU HAVE BEEN IN THE SITUATION AND HAD THE EXPERIENCE, THEN HE SHOULD KEEP HIS MOUTH SHUT, FIRMLY SHUT."

Ferguson offers his warm congratulations to Wenger for getting the top job at Arsenal.

"IT'S WRONG THE LEAGUE PROGRAMME IS EXTENDED SO UNITED CAN REST UP AND WIN EVERYTHING,"

suggests Wenger when Premier League fixtures were moved to accommodate Manchester United challenging multiple titles and trophies.

105

"HE'S AT A BIG CLUB – WELL, ARSENAL USED TO BE A BIG CLUB – AND MAYBE NEXT YEAR HE COULD BE IN THE SAME SITUATION. I WONDER WHAT HIS STORY WILL BE THEN?"
Ferguson underscores his maturity by suggesting he's got the bigger one.

"EVERYONE THINKS THEY HAVE THE PRETTIEST WIFE AT HOME,"
said Wenger when Ferguson suggested that his third-placed Manchester United were playing better football than the first-placed Arsenal.

"TO NOT APOLOGISE FOR THE BEHAVIOUR OF THE PLAYERS TO ANOTHER MANAGER IS UNTHINKABLE. IT'S A DISGRACE, BUT I DON'T EXPECT WENGER TO EVER APOLOGISE … HE'S THAT TYPE OF PERSON."
Ferguson scrambles for the moral high ground.

"WE HAVE LOADS OF SITUATIONS NOW WHERE NEW MANAGERS COME IN AND VANISH AFTER A COUPLE OF YEARS. IT'S JUST THE TWO OF US AND WE'LL PROBABLY RIDE OUT INTO THE SUNSET TOGETHER,"
said Ferguson on his improved relationship with Wenger in 2009. More unlikely bromance films have been made …

"IT WAS SOMETIMES VERY AGGRESSIVE, ESPECIALLY AFTER THE GAMES. WHEN YOU'RE FIGHTING TO WIN, YOU ARE TWO LIONS,"
said the Frenchman about the Scot.

"FERGUSON'S OUT OF ORDER. HE HAS LOST ALL SENSE OF REALITY. HE IS GOING OUT LOOKING FOR A CONFRONTATION, THEN ASKING THE PERSON HE IS CONFRONTING TO APOLOGISE. HE'S PUSHED THE CORK IN A BIT FAR THIS TIME,"
suggested Wenger after a pizza somehow ended up flying through the air in the tunnel and hitting Ferguson after another hotly contested match between Arsenal and Manchester United.

"WHAT I DON'T UNDERSTAND IS THAT HE DOES WHAT HE WANTS AND YOU ARE ALL AT HIS FEET."
Wenger reflects on Ferguson's relationship with the press. Something something, seagull follows the trawler, something something.

"IT BECAME TOXIC FOR A WHILE."
Ferguson reflects on his relationship with Arsène Wenger.

★ DENNIS BERGKAMP ★

Dennis Bergkamp combined the finesse of football in the Netherlands with the strength and power of the English game. He became a devastating addition to Arsenal's front line when he joined the club in 1995.

It's a funny old thing now that you look back at it, but while Bergkamp was seen as a bright prospect at Ajax, he was not particularly rated as a footballer when he first emerged on the scene. He struggled in Italy during his two years at Inter Milan, and he took his time acclimatising to the way that the game is played in England, going without scoring in his first seven games in north London.

But then along comes Arsène Wenger, bringing with him continental strategies that had been finessed for the way that the game was played in England. Bergkamp never really looked back, and his combination of tricksy, feather-light touch and devastating power was central to Arsenal's success in the late 1990s and early 2000s. He made 423 appearances for the Gunners, scoring 120 times, winning the FA Cup four times and the Premier League and FA Charity/Community Shield three times each. He also gained the nickname 'the Non-Flying Dutchman' as a result of his contract clause excusing him from aeroplane travel, due to an extreme phobia of flying.

GOING THROUGH
★ CHANGES ★

The rules of football were first written down in 1863 at the Freemasons' Tavern in Blackheath, not far from Woolwich. It was an attempt to bring consistency to a game that was previously played in several different ways, depending on where you found yourself. Twelve clubs and schools from across the capital and its surrounding suburbs were represented at that first meeting, forming the Football Association and making a decent start down the road to making football what it is today.

They appear to have got the basics right, with the standardised game quickly being picked up and popularised in the north, before bouncing back to the south with the emergence of teams like Arsenal two decades later. Not that there are any teams like Arsenal.

Over the years there have been numerous changes to the rules. Corner kicks were not a thing until 1872, goal kicks didn't arrive in the rule book until 1890, and crossbars weren't compulsory until 1875. Referees didn't get whistles until 1878.

Penalties weren't introduced until 1891, purely coincidentally around the point that England's dominance in world football started to diminish. The penalty spot itself wasn't introduced for another 11 years. Before that, penalties could be taken anywhere along a 12-yard line (a 10.97-metre line, if you were wondering). This is why they were somewhat threateningly called 'kicks of death' rather than 'spot kicks' back in the olden days.

The offside rule has changed more times than the funky little table that sits in the middle of the *Match of the Day* set. There's traditionally a day in mid-October when commentators finally understand how it's changed, and analysis by artificial intelligence shows that, on average, football supporters don't get their heads around it until at least 37 days later. You can hear a sigh from the terraces in late November after the ref's blown up for offside when everyone finally gets it. And then they change the rules again 196 days later.

Even now, the rules are evolving, and they are likely to

keep evolving for as long as the game is played. Some of the changes will be good, and some will cause endless debate and irritation. But think on this: if there were no more rule changes, what would the pundits have to give their opinions about in the post-match analysis after a 0–0 draw? You can't take away all of their fun. It's how they justify getting a new little table.

ARSENAL HAVE NEVER BEEN RELEGATED, BUT WOOLWICH ARSENAL DIPPED DOWN INTO THE SECOND DIVISION IN 1913.

THE ONE THING I
DIDN'T EXPECT IS THE
WAY WE DIDN'T PLAY.

George Graham

★ PATRICK VIEIRA ★

Patrick Vieira owned the midfield and was a joy to watch. He joined Arsenal in 1996, making 279 League appearances during a nine year, double-double 'Invincibles'-winning stint with the club. He appears to have been central to Arsène Wenger's plans for the club right from the start, with an agreement to sign the player in place before Wenger had formally taken the manager's position.

Vieira brought power and delicacy to his midfield role, effortlessly holding off defenders and picking out the perfect pass. It was a joy to watch – unless you were playing for a different team. He was a constant threat that enhanced Arsenal's suite of weapons.

He took the captain's armband when Tony Adams retired in 2002, taking the responsibility of leading his team seriously and respectfully while continuing to give the Gunners a variety of options whenever they surged forward.

He also enjoyed significant success with the French national team as part of the World Cup winning squad in 1998, the Euros in 2000 and the Confederations Cup in 2001.

He left Arsenal in 2005, joining first Juventus, then Inter Milan before rounding out a storied career with a stint at Manchester City. He subsequently went into management, initially with the Manchester City-linked New York City FC, then Nice and Crystal Palace.

Vieira was at the centre of one of the greatest teams of the Premier League, if not the entire history of football. Finding a replacement was exceedingly difficult.

ARSENAL WERE THE FIRST ENGLISH TEAM TO NAME A FULL SQUAD OF FOREIGN PLAYERS, INCLUDING SUBSTITUTES, WHEN THEY MET CRYSTAL PALACE EARLY IN 2005. THE GUNNERS WON 5-1.

"WHEN PATRICK VIEIRA FIRST CAME FROM AC MILAN, HE DIDN'T KNOW A WORD OF ENGLISH. WE GAVE HIM ACCOMMODATION, PHONE, CAR AND AN ENGLISH TEACHER. I TALKED TO PATRICK IN FLUENT FRENCH AND BEFORE A GAME I ASKED IN FRENCH, 'COULD YOU SPEAK A LITTLE BIT OF ENGLISH TO ME?' PATRICK NODDED AND REPLIED, 'TOTTENHAM ARE SHIT'."

Former vice-chairman David Dein does his bit for north London diplomacy.

Season	Goals	
2002/03	Thierry Henry	24
2003/04	Thierry Henry	30
2004/05	Thierry Henry	25
2005/06	Thierry Henry	27
2006/07	Robin van Persie	11
2007/08	Emmanuel Adebayor	24
2008/09	Robin van Persie	11
2009/10	Cesc Fàbregas	15
2010/11	Robin van Persie	18
2011/12	Robin van Persie	30
2012/13	Theo Walcott	14
2013/14	Olivier Giroud	16
2014/15	Alexis Sánchez	16
2015/16	Olivier Giroud	16
2016/17	Alexis Sánchez	24
2017/18	Alexandre Lacazette	14
2018/19	Pierre-Emerick Aubameyang	22
2019/20	Pierre-Emerick Aubameyang	22
2020/21	Alexandre Lacazette	13
2021/22	Bukayo Saka	11
2022/23	Martin Ødergaard/ Gabriel Martinelli	15

Goals   0   5   10

ARSENAL'S LEADING GOAL SCORERS ★ BY SEASON ★

(ALL COMPETITIONS)

15   20   25   30   35   40   45

★ EMMANUEL PETIT ★

Life is too short to obsess about getting one over on your rivals. The grown-up thing to do is let your performances speak for themselves, whether that's on the football pitch, in the workplace or in any other sphere of human endeavour. That said, if the opportunity does arise, it's rude not to grab it with both hands.

Emmanuel Petit was a central midfielder at Monaco who came to London to talk about a possible move to Spurs in 1997. The meeting went well, by all accounts, but Petit asked for the opportunity to think over his decision, and so the Spurs leadership very kindly got him a taxi back to his hotel.

Once in the car, Petit redirected the driver to Arsène Wenger's home, where his old manager convinced him that he should join the Gunners rather than Spurs. Which he duly did, forming a formidable three-season defensive partnership with Patrick Vieira that helped Arsenal clinch the double in 1997/98.

Arsenal owes Tottenham a debt of gratitude. And, technically, the cost of that taxi ride.

ARSENAL HAVE WON THE
FA CUP 14 TIMES, BUT THEY
HAVE ALSO BEEN RUNNERS-
UP SEVEN TIMES, ALONGSIDE
LIVERPOOL AND NEWCASTLE
UNITED. CHELSEA, EVERTON AND
MANCHESTER UNITED HAVE
COME SECOND EIGHT TIMES.

YOU SAY 'FOOTBALL', ★ I SAY 'SOCCER' ★

Most people in Britain who follow football go very quiet when an American comes along and calls the beautiful game 'soccer'. A few get visibly upset. "It's not right," they cry. "Why do they call their version of rugby 'football', when the ball is actually very rarely kicked, and the actual game of football, where 20 of the 22 players on the pitch can only touch the ball with their feet, 'soccer'?"

"It makes no sense," they say, "and the Americans need to wise up ..."

There are two big problems with this argument: firstly, the Americans really don't care; and secondly, the Americans are less wrong than you might imagine. Because 'soccer' is an English term.

A long time ago, long before the rules of football were standardised, in a time when knights still roamed the land, there were basically two types of sport. There was sport that was played by the aristocracy, who had horses and played noble sports on horseback; and there were sports played by the hoi polloi, the common folk, who moved around on the ground and mostly kicked balls.

As a result, all sports that weren't played on horseback were called 'football'. There weren't any governing bodies or standardised rules – everything was just lumped together as football. (It could have been worse, it could have been called 'commonfolkrunningaroundamusingthemselvesaren'ttheyfoolswhydon'ttheybuyhorsesandplaypropersports?')

In 1823, the game of 'rugby football' was invented at a posh school who's name no one can remember. It became the first type of football played on the ground that had clearly defined rules and was played consistently across the country. This is why if you look at most of the older rugby teams, they list themselves as rugby football teams.

A few years later, people thought that it would be good to do a similar thing with another type of football, so they sat down, created some rules and a governing body. They called it 'association football', which is why some of the older football teams call themselves association football teams.

In the nature of language, particularly when it moves from south to north, people started to realise that association football was a bit of a mouthful, and it began to transmute into 'assoc' and then 'soccer'. Meanwhile, the same process was taking place in the odd-shaped ball community, and Brits started to drop the word 'football' when they were talking about rugby football. This freed up the word 'football' to be used by the round-shaped ball community, so the word 'soccer' fell out of fashion and we ended up with two games: football and rugby.

Before this process was completed, though, association football made its way across the north Atlantic. But over there, they continued to call football 'soccer' because American football was already established and no one wanted to go through the rigmarole of changing the name of the sport to what it should technically be, which is probably American Rules Rugby Football (ARRF).

So, next time you hear someone talking about soccer, rather than quietly wincing or getting into a row, simply nod and accept that it is what it is: they are not historically incorrect, and there is a fairly reasonable argument to say that it is actually more incorrect to shorten 'association football' to 'football'.

Ultimately, we face a choice: we can either waste our precious time on this planet getting upset about something that isn't completely wrong and certainly isn't going to change, or we can gather together all the rugby (both codes), American football, Aussie rules and football association governing bodies from around the world and get them to sit down over a nice cup of tea and discuss a reasonable compromise. This would need to involve developing a globally consistent naming protocol for all relevant sports that was logical, culturally appropriate, historically correct and not going to annoy anyone.

It might be easier to just accept that the world is slightly wonky and get on with enjoying the world's second most popular sport, whether you call it 'football' or 'soccer'.

"A TEAM CAN ATTACK FOR TOO LONG. THE MOST OPPORTUNE TIME FOR SCORING IS IMMEDIATELY AFTER REPELLING AN ATTACK, BECAUSE OPPONENTS ARE THEN STRUNG OUT IN THE WRONG HALF OF THE FIELD. ALL THE MEN ARE EXPECTED TO PLAY TO PLAN, BUT NOT SO AS TO STIFLE INDIVIDUALITY."

Herbert Chapman.

★ ASHLEY COLE ★

For every Sol Campbell, who arrived at Highbury in what our neighbours down the road would call 'controversial circumstances', there is an Ashley Cole, who left Arsenal for Chelsea under something of a cloud.

During his time with the Gunners, he won the Premier League in 2001/02 and 2003/04, and the FA Cup in 2002, 2003 and 2005. In total he made 228 first team appearances for the Gunners, scoring nine goals and generally being a stalwart of the defensive line.

The trouble came when he was caught meeting with senior officials from Chelsea without informing Arsenal, where he was still under contract. It was a fairly ugly incident and no one really came out with much dignity, but it's worth remembering that Arsenal were the team that Cole followed as a boy, and what we read in the papers is not always the full story.

Player	Club
Michael Owen	Liverpool, Newcastle United, Manchester United, Stoke City
Jermain Defoe	Bournemouth, Sunderland, Tottenham Hotspur, Portsmouth, West Ham, Charlton Athletic
Robbie Fowler	Liverpool, Leeds, Manchester City, Blackburn Rovers
Thierry Henry	Arsenal
Frank Lampard	West Ham, Chelsea, Manchester City
Sergio Agüero	Manchester City
Andrew Cole	Sunderland, Portsmouth, Manchester City, Fulham, Blackburn Rovers, Manchester United, Newcastle United
Wayne Rooney	Everton, Manchester United
Harry Kane	Tottenham Hotspur
Alan Shearer	Blackburn Rovers, Newcastle United

PREMIER LEAGUE'S
★ TOP SCORERS ★

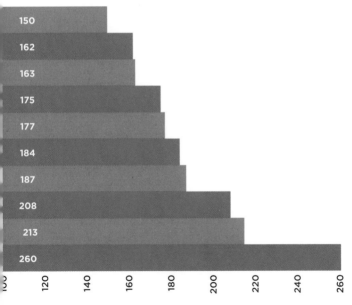

150
162
163
175
177
184
187
208
213
260

120 140 160 180 200 220 240 260

"IT STICKS IN THE CRAW BECAUSE NOBODY LIKES THE ARSENAL, BUT YOU SIMPLY CAN'T HELP BUT ENJOY WATCHING THE FOOTBALL THEY PLAY."

The notoriously vocal Brian Clough says it as it is.

"NICOLAS ANELKA LEFT ARSENAL FOR £23 MILLION AND THEY BUILT A TRAINING GROUND ON HIM."

Kevin Keegan explains why nobody heard of Anelka after he left Highbury.

THEY WERE ONLY
★ BEING SPURSY ... ★

Recently, St Totteringham's Day has not been celebrated as regularly as it was at the turn of the millennium, but while Spurs are doing better than they were, they still often seem to trip over themselves in the most entertaining fashion. Fighting for a Champions League place in the last game of the season? Three-quarters of the team go down with a virus. 2–0 up in a match against Chelsea to keep title hopes alive? Implode in the most spectacular fashion in the second half, draw the match and receive a hefty fine for brawling.

Imagine having world-beating talent on the pitch, getting yourself into phenomenal positions and finding yourself standing in front of an open goal. You are going to do it, you are going to do it ... it's harder to miss than hit ... and then you watch the ball go sailing over the bar. It is a special skill that Tottenham have displayed several times over the last few years, and some people have come up with a word for it: it's called being 'Spursy'. "They were just being a bit Spursy," you say with a shrug and a little chuckle.

There was a rumour that the word 'Spursy' was going to be added to the Oxford English Dictionary in 2016. Those rumours presumably came from somewhere in N5 rather than N17.

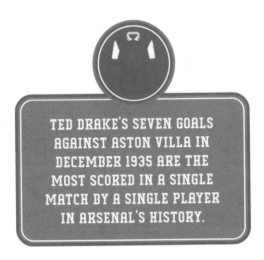

TED DRAKE'S SEVEN GOALS AGAINST ASTON VILLA IN DECEMBER 1935 ARE THE MOST SCORED IN A SINGLE MATCH BY A SINGLE PLAYER IN ARSENAL'S HISTORY.

TRIANGULAR
★ CORNER FLAGS ★

When you look at football grounds around the country, sometimes you notice small differences. For example, most teams in England use rectangular corner flags but, particularly when it comes to the FA Cup, some use triangular flags.

This is because there is a convention that only teams that have won the FA Cup have the right to use triangular flags. This is said to have emanated from South Wales, where Cardiff started using triangular flags to remind local rivals Swansea that they had won the cup in 1927 (by beating Arsenal – but it's not really worth holding it against them; they've won it three times and Arsenal have won it 14 times).

Using triangular flags to mark FA cup winners caught on, and they are now used by several other teams that have lifted the trophy, including Arsenal, Aston Villa, Chelsea, Everton, Preston North End and AFC Wimbledon (based on their association with Wimbledon) and presumably the Old Etonians (who won in 1878/79 and 1881/82).

The thing is, though, there's nothing in any of the sport's rule books that says that FA Cup winners must, or even have the right, to use triangular flags, so it's a convention rather than a rule. From the sound of things, it tends to be a question of the groundkeeper's discretion, with several FA Cup winners, including Liverpool, sticking with the standard rectangular flags, often because when teams are on a run they don't like to change anything.

The rule book only really states that corner flags have to be there and can't be used for advertising, so presumably a corner flag could be an octagon if that happened to take the groundkeeper's fancy. Sounds silly, but it'll happen one day.

★ THIERRY HENRY ★

Thierry Henry's arrival at Highbury was a relatively muted affair. He was clearly an exciting talent, having been named French Young Footballer of the Year for his contributions to Monaco in 1996/97 and been part of the French team that won the 1998 World Cup. But his subsequent move to Italy to join Juventus, plying his trade down the left wing, only delivered moderate success.

He joined Arsenal in 1999 for £11 million, and Wenger quickly set to work bringing Henry in from the wing to become a striker to replace the recently departed Nicolas Anelka. He took his time settling, going eight games without scoring ... and then delivering 17 Premier League goals over the rest of the season.

That was the start of what is probably fair to call a glittering career with Arsenal. He slotted home another 17 Premier League goals in 2000/01, 24 the year after and the year after that, 30 in 2003/04, 25 in 2004/05, 27 in 2005/06, before delivering 10 more in 2006/07. In total, he helped deliver the Premier League in 2001/02 and 2003/04, the FA Cup in 2001/02 and 2002/03 and the FA Community Shield in both 2002 and 2004. He was also central to the teams that came second in the UEFA

Champions League in 2005/06 and the UEFA Cup in 1999/2000.

After all that, he decided to go and take it easy in Spain. He helped Barcelona win La Liga in 2008/09 and 2009/10, the Copa del Rey in 2008/09, the Supercopa de España in 2009, the UEFA Champions League in 2008/09, the UEFA Super Cup in 2009 and the FIFA Club World Cup in 2009. Which is not half bad.

There were several reasons why he moved on from Arsenal. One of which was a change of chairman and the start of questions about whether Wenger was going to move on, but also he was starting to feel that his verbal approach to the game, coupled with his legendary status, was potentially hindering the team. Basically, people would pass him the ball whenever he shouted for it – even if there were other players in better positions. We've all been there.

He returned to Arsenal briefly in the 2011/12 season, arriving on loan for a couple of months from America as cover for players that were away participating in the Africa Cup of Nations. He added another couple of goals to his tally, meaning that he ended his career with Arsenal having scored 228 goals, 175 of them in the Premier League.

"ARSENAL IS IN MY BLOOD AS WELL AS MY HEART. I WILL ALWAYS, ALWAYS, ALWAYS REMEMBER YOU GUYS. I SAID I WAS GOING TO BE A GOONER FOR LIFE AND I DID NOT LIE BECAUSE WHEN YOU ARE A GOONER, YOU WILL ALWAYS BE A GOONER. THIS CLUB IS IN MY HEART AND WILL REMAIN IN MY HEART FOREVER."

When Thierry Henry expresses his emotions, he always leaves room for interpretation.

THE BATTLE OF
★ HIGHBURY ★

This is a book about Arsenal, so the exploits of the English national team are technically only of passing interest, but the November 1934 match between England and Italy is a little different. For a start, it took place at Highbury, but it also featured seven Arsenal players - a record number from one club that stands even today.

Italy were football's World Champions, but England, alongside the other British national teams, had walked away from FIFA in 1928 in a dispute over payments to amateur players. Despite this, England were still considered to be a very strong footballing nation and, as a result, the match was widely billed as the 'real' World Cup final – in England at least. This was part of the reason why there were 56,000 people on the terraces to witness what was, by all accounts, a pretty unpleasant spectacle. A friendly it was not.

England did not seem to take the match massively seriously, though, with none of its players having more than 10 caps. For Italy, however, it was seen as an opportunity to show the world that they were the true masters of world football, with Italian dictator Benito Mussolini promising each Italian player a brand-new Alfa Romeo if they won the match. Whether this was actually an incentive is anybody's guess.

England went ahead with an early goal to make up for missing a penalty a few moments before, and that, from the sounds of things was pretty much the end of the match from a footballing point of view. An Italian player went into a challenge with Ted Drake and broke his own foot. This was before substitutes had been invented, so he tried to play on, but England scored twice before Italy got their plan B in order.

The second half saw the visitors get their heads together and put together two quick-fire goals, but England somehow found a way to hold on and the match ended 3–2. Among the list of people who hobbled off the pitch at the end of the match, Drake is reported to have had two black eyes, a swollen jaw and a leg that was said to have been nearly cut to ribbons. Manchester City's Eric Brook had his arm broken. Eddie Hapgood had his nose broken and had to leave the field to have it reset.

It is worth pointing out that the Italian team also came off the pitch with their fair share of injuries as a result of plenty of two-footed challenges and robust shoulder barges from the English – so perhaps we should be a little careful about pointing fingers. Not least because they might get accidentally snapped off.

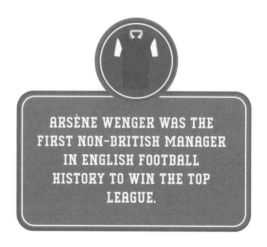

ARSÈNE WENGER WAS THE
FIRST NON-BRITISH MANAGER
IN ENGLISH FOOTBALL
HISTORY TO WIN THE TOP
LEAGUE.

"THEN YOU HAVE
TO CONVINCE THE
PLAYERS AND GET
THEM ON BOARD WITH
WHAT YOU ARE DOING,
AND AFTER THAT YOU
CAN START TO BUILD.
BUT THE IDENTITY IS
THE FOUNDATION FOR
EVERYTHING,"

observes Mikel Arteta, architect
of Arsenal's renaissance.

Player	Club
Bryan Robson	West Bromwich Albion, Manchester United, Middlesborough
Billy Wright	Wolverhampton Wanderers
Frank Lampard	West Ham, Chelsea, Manchester City
Bobby Charlton	Manchester United
Ashley Cole	Arsenal, Chelsea, Derby County
Bobby Moore	West Ham, Fulham
Steven Gerrard	Liverpool
David Beckham	Manchester United
Wayne Rooney	Everton, Manchester United, Derby County
Peter Shilton	Leicester City, Stoke City, Nottingham Forest, Southampton, Derby County, Plymouth Argyle, Wimbledon, Bolton Wanderers, Coventry City, West Ham United, Leyton Orient

Caps

ENGLAND CAPS CHART

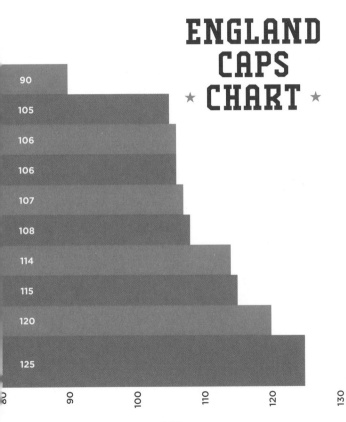

	Caps
	90
	105
	106
	106
	107
	108
	114
	115
	120
	125

80   90   100   110   120   130

★ SOL CAMPBELL ★

Sol Campbell's career started relatively late when he joined Arsenal for the 2001/02 season. He'd apparently dabbled in football a bit elsewhere in London, but it was at Highbury that he really shone. In a glittering five years at the club, he won the Premier League in 2001/02 and 2003/04, the FA Cup in 2001/02, 2002–03 and 2004–05, the FA Community Shield in 2002 and was a UEFA Champions League runner-up in 2005/06.

A robust defender, he'd caught Arsène Wenger's eye because he had an ability to see and block attacks before they happened, and his partnership with Kolo Touré was the foundation that the 'Invincibles' season was built on.

He left the club at the end of the 2005/06 season, although he returned briefly in 2009/10. He also enjoyed a long career with the England team, playing active roles at every international tournament between Euro 1996 and the 2006 World Cup. In 1998, Campbell became the Three Lion's second-youngest ever captain (after Bobby Moore).

"I LIKED A FIGHT AND
ALWAYS STOOD UP
FOR MYSELF. THAT'S
HOW I WAS BROUGHT
UP. COMING FROM
HOLLOWAY YOU LEARN
FROM THE PRAM TO
NUT PEOPLE WHO PICK
ON YOU."

Charlie George.

"THE GAME IS BALANCED IN ARSENAL'S FAVOUR,"

observes John Motson, explaining the way that it should always be.

THE OPPOSITION: ★ LIVERPOOL ★

Arsenal and Liverpool have a deeply professional rivalry. There's no massive animosity, but there's an expectation between both sets of fans that their teams will play beautiful football that has them somewhere near the top league at the end of each season, and the two teams know that there is a decent chance it will be a tough game.

What this translates to is that even when they are not competing for the very top position in the Premier League, they tend to be challenging each other for Champions League spots. Given the heritage that both teams have in Europe, their meetings tend to be fairly high stakes.

This may go some way to explaining why the two teams have delivered just under three goals on average during the more than 60 times that they have clashed in the Premier League. There have only been five 0–0 draws since 1992, which means you are as likely to see goals between Arsenal and Liverpool as you are in a north London derby and, proving that statistics are fun, the number of goals that you are likely to see is 0.12 higher on average between Arsenal and Liverpool than Arsenal and Tottenham. Stick that in your pub quiz.

Arsenal beat Liverpool 40% of the time, while the Reds win just over 25% of the time. That's not a bad statistic, but if you drill down into the home and away figures, Arsenal win 53% of the time at Anfield but win less than 30% of the time at home. Make of that what you will.

★ MIKEL ARTETA ★

The thing about Arsenal fans is that they have short memories and an assumption that they will win everything every time. This can make managing expectations exceptionally difficult. Case in point: Mikel Arteta.

Arteta joined Arsenal in 2011 and played a key role in keeping the team in contention for five years, as well as helping Arsenal win the FA Cup and the Community Shield in 2014. He made 110 league appearances for Arsenal, scoring 14 goals.

Although he played a regular role in Spanish international youth teams, he never made the transition to full international, held out by a mixture of injuries and other players in what was seen as a golden generation.

On retiring from football, he appears to have had the choice of staying with Arsenal to coach the Academy, join the backroom staff at Tottenham or link up with Pep Guardiola, who he had known back in his academy days at Barcelona, at the newly emergent Manchester City. He chose the latter, and while there, Arteta was involved in helping City win two Premier League titles, an FA Cup, and two EFL Cups between 2015 and 2019.

He took over at Arsenal mid-way through the 2019/20

season, guiding them past both Manchester City and Chelsea to lift the FA Cup, which he followed with victory over Liverpool in the FA Community Shield a month later. It seemed like a legend could be being born.

The next season was more troubled, though, with Arsenal finishing eighth for the second consecutive year, but this time they didn't get past the fourth round of the FA Cup, meaning that they failed to qualify for the Champions League for the first time in quarter of a century.

With a shaky start to the 2021/22 season, there were considerable rumblings of discontent at the Emirates Stadium, but Arteta looked at the problems, dealt with them, got on with his job and slowly it became clear that he was building something positive. Arsenal started the 2022/23 season well and Arsenal quickly scrambled to the top of the league ...

Coming second at any time is distressing, but coming second after leading the league for so long is absolutely heart-breaking. But let's not dwell on that, let's celebrate the team that Arteta's put together and the way he's got them playing. On to the next season, we go again ...

"BEHIND EVERY GREAT GOALKEEPER THERE'S A BALL FROM IAN WRIGHT."

So proclaimed a Nike advert from the 1990s. It wasn't wrong.

★ ALEX SCOTT ★

Alex Scott came through the Arsenal youth system, starting out as a striker or right-winger before evolving into a right back. She never lost sight of goal, though, and was always quick to get the ball into attacking positions. She joined Birmingham City for the 2004/05 season, helping them finish a decent fourth at the top level of the women's game in England, but moved back to Arsenal when Birmingham found themselves in financial difficulties. She helped the Arsenal team deliver a string of titles and trophies over the next four years.

Scott moved to the US in 2009 to join the Boston Breakers but returned to Arsenal in 2012 when the Women's Professional Soccer league collapsed. She became the Gunner's captain for the 2014/15 season, helping add to an already bulging trophy cabinet. In total, she won 21 titles with Arsenal during her three stints with the club.

She also made 140 appearances for England, and was part of the team representing Great Britain at the 2012 London Olympics.

Since putting her playing career behind her she has built a successful media career with several broadcasters.

THE
★ TROPHY CABINET ★

Competition	Year
First Division Premier League	1930/31, 1932/33, 1933/34, 1934/35, 1937/38, 1947/48, 1952/53, 1970/71, 1988/89, 1990/91, 1997/98, 2001/02, 2003/04
FA Cup	1929/30, 1935/36, 1949/50, 1970/71, 1978/79, 1992/93, 1997/98, 2001/02, 2002/03, 2004/05, 2013/14, 2014/15, 2016/17, 2019/20
Football League Cup EFL Cup	1986/87, 1992/93
FA Charity Shield FA Community Shield	1930, 1931, 1933, 1934, 1938, 1948, 1953, 1991 (shared), 1998, 1999, 2002, 2004, 2014, 2015, 2017, 2020
Inter-Cities Fairs Cup	1969/70
European Cup Winners' Cup	1993/94